STATE PROFILES

OHIO

BY BETSY RATHBURN

BELLWETHER MEDIA • MINNEAPOLIS, MN

Blastoff! Discovery launches a new mission: reading to learn. Filled with facts and features, each book offers you an exciting new world to explore!

BLASTOFF! UNIVERSE

BLASTOFF! Beginners — GRADE K

BLASTOFF! READERS — GRADES 1-3

BLASTOFF! DISCOVERY — GRADE 4

This edition first published in 2022 by Bellwether Media, Inc.

No part of this publication may be reproduced in whole or in part without written permission of the publisher.
For information regarding permission, write to Bellwether Media, Inc., Attention: Permissions Department,
6012 Blue Circle Drive, Minnetonka, MN 55343.

Library of Congress Cataloging-in-Publication Data

Names: Rathburn, Betsy, author.
Title: Ohio / Betsy by Rathburn.
Description: Minneapolis, MN : Bellwether Media, 2022. | Series: Blastoff! Discovery: State Profiles | Includes bibliographical references and index. | Audience: Ages 7-13 | Audience: Grades 4-6 | Summary: "Engaging images accompany information about Ohio. The combination of high-interest subject matter and narrative text is intended for students in grades 3 through 8" – Provided by publisher.
Identifiers: LCCN 2021020860 (print) | LCCN 2021020861 (ebook) | ISBN 9781644873403 (library binding) | ISBN 9781648341830 (ebook)
Subjects: LCSH: Ohio–Juvenile literature.
Classification: LCC F491.3 .R38 2022 (print) | LCC F491.3 (ebook) | DDC 977.1–dc23
LC record available at https://lccn.loc.gov/2021020860
LC ebook record available at https://lccn.loc.gov/2021020861

Editor: Kate Moening   Designer: Laura Sowers

Printed in the United States of America, North Mankato, MN.

TABLE OF CONTENTS

CedarPoint

ASH CAVE
HOCKING HILL STATE PARK

A family is visiting Hocking Hills State Park. This popular park has many **distinct** areas. The family plans to hike to the popular Ash Cave. They start down a path through a narrow **gorge**. Poplar, oak, and hemlock trees shade the trail. In their branches, worm-eating warblers and blue-headed vireos chirp and sing.

OLD MAN'S CAVE

Old Man's Cave is a popular part of Hocking Hills State Park. It is named for a man called Richard Rowe. He lived in the cave in the late 1700s!

CEDAR POINT

CUYAHOGA VALLEY NATIONAL PARK

GREAT SERPENT MOUND

ROCK AND ROLL HALL OF FAME

Soon, the family steps into Ash Cave. Soft sand covers the ground. Stone walls tower above. The family looks up to see a thin waterfall tumbling over the rim of the gorge. It drops into a small, clear pool. Welcome to Ohio!

WHERE IS OHIO?

Ohio is a heart-shaped state that covers 44,826 square miles (116,099 square kilometers) of the Midwest. It is the 34th largest state. Its capital city, Columbus, is in the center of the state.

To the west, Ohio shares its long, straight border with Indiana. Michigan is to the northwest. Lake Erie makes up Ohio's northeastern edge. The city of Cleveland sits on its shores. Pennsylvania is Ohio's eastern neighbor. The Ohio River separates Ohio from West Virginia in the southeast and Kentucky in the south. The city of Cincinnati lies on the Kentucky border.

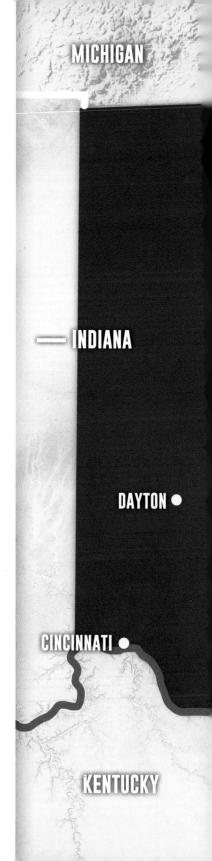

MICHIGAN

— INDIANA

DAYTON ●

CINCINNATI ●

KENTUCKY

N
W ✚ E
S

TOLEDO

LAKE ERIE

● CLEVELAND

● AKRON

PENNSYLVANIA —

OHIO

★ COLUMBUS

OHIO
RIVER

WEST VIRGINIA

THE HEART OF IT ALL

Ohio is often called "the heart of it all." This is because of the state's shape. It is also because there is a lot to do in Ohio!

OHIO'S BEGINNINGS

QUEEN ALIQUIPPA
OF THE SENECA

People have lived in Ohio for thousands of years. The Adena and Hopewell built huge mounds that still stand today! In the 1600s, Iroquois groups pushed other tribes out of Ohio. They wanted control over the booming fur trade with Dutch and British settlers. Some Native Americans, such as the Shawnee, returned by the early 1700s.

GREAT RIVER, GREAT NAME

Ohio's name comes from an Iroquois word that means "great river."

Soon, the French took over the area. But they quickly lost control of Ohio to the British. In 1783, the British lost the Revolutionary War. This made Ohio part of the United States. It became the 17th state in 1803.

NATIVE PEOPLES OF OHIO

Ohio has no government-recognized tribes in the state today.

OTTAWA

- Original lands in eastern Canada and Michigan, then northern Ohio
- Descendants largely in Oklahoma, Michigan, and Ontario, Canada
- Also called Odawa and Odaawaa

WYANDOT

- Original lands in southern Ontario, Canada, then northern Ohio
- Descendants largely in Oklahoma, Kansas, Michigan, and Quebec, Canada
- Also called Wendat and Huron

MIAMI

- Original lands in Indiana, Illinois, Michigan, and Ohio
- Descendants largely in the Miami Tribe of Oklahoma
- Also called Myaamia

SHAWNEE

- Original lands in southern Ohio
- Descendants largely in Oklahoma

SENECA AND CAYUGA

- Original lands in New York and Pennsylvania, then northern Ohio
- Descendants largely in the Seneca-Cayuga Nation in Oklahoma

LANDSCAPE AND CLIMATE

Ohio is on the western edge of the Appalachian Mountains. Much of the state's eastern land is part of the Appalachian **Plateau**. This area has rolling hills in the north and steeper slopes to the south. **Plains** cover western Ohio. These extend from Lake Erie in the north to the Ohio River in the south.

LAKE ERIE

OHIO RIVER

APPALACHIAN PLATEAU

N
W — E
S

OHIO'S CHALLENGE: CLEAN AIR NEEDED

Air pollution is a serious problem in Ohio. Cincinnati and Cleveland are among the most polluted cities in the country. Coal factories make air pollution worse. Not addressing this issue will make people and animals sick.

OHIO RIVER

SPRING
HIGH: 60°F (16°C)
LOW: 39°F (4°C)

SUMMER
HIGH: 81°F (27°C)
LOW: 61°F (16°C)

FALL
HIGH: 62°F (17°C)
LOW: 44°F (7°C)

WINTER
HIGH: 37°F (3°C)
LOW: 21°F (-6°C)

°F = degrees Fahrenheit
°C = degrees Celsius

OHIO BUCKEYE

Ohio's state tree is the Ohio buckeye tree. Buckeyes are known for their dark brown nuts. The buckeye nut is a common symbol of Ohio!

Ohio has a continental climate. Spring is rainy. It sometimes brings thunderstorms and tornadoes. Summer is hot and humid, while fall is mild. Winter is cold and snowy, especially in the north. Heavy snowstorms often hit Lake Erie during this season.

VIRGINIA OPOSSUM

Ohio is full of wildlife! Hungry bobcats and gray foxes hunt in forests for prey. They share the land with white-tailed deer. Bright northern cardinals add color to the trees. Rabbits and squirrels scurry through yards. Beavers build dams in Ohio's lakes and streams. They swim alongside trout, bass, and many other fish!

After dark, star-nosed moles and opossums come out to search for food. Ohio's night sky is full of animals, too. Clover looper moths flutter near porch lights. Big brown bats swoop and dive to catch them.

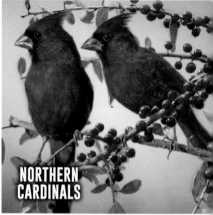

NORTHERN CARDINALS

WHITE-TAILED DEER

BOBCAT

CLOVER LOOPER MOTH

GRAY FOX

Life Span: up to 8 years
Status: least concern

gray fox range = ▪

LEAST CONCERN	NEAR THREATENED	VULNERABLE	ENDANGERED	CRITICALLY ENDANGERED	EXTINCT IN THE WILD	EXTINCT
▲						

Nearly 12 million people call Ohio home. About three out of four Ohioans live in **urban** areas. Most Ohioans have **ancestors** from Europe. Black or African Americans are the second-largest **ethnic** group, followed by people with Hispanic and Asian backgrounds.

AMISH COUNTRY

Around 60,000 Amish people live in Ohio. They are known for their simple lifestyle that does not include modern technology.

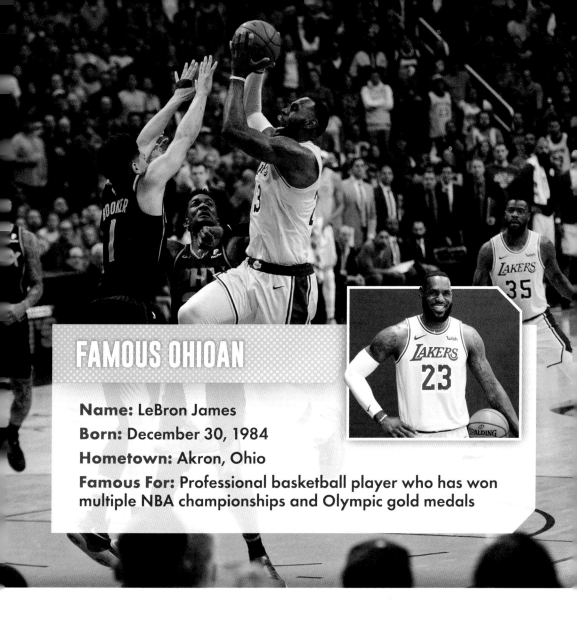

Over 500,000 immigrants live in Ohio. In recent years, most have come from Mexico, India, China, the Philippines, and Canada. Ohio also has a small population of Native Americans. Many of their ancestors were forced to leave for reservations in the 1800s. Today, Native American Ohioans live in the state's towns and cities.

Columbus is in the center of Ohio. The city was founded in 1812. Four years later, it became Ohio's capital. Columbus sits at the **confluence** of the Olentangy and Scioto Rivers. Its location made trade and travel easier for early settlers.

Today, about 900,000 people live in Columbus. Many people live and work downtown. People also gather downtown for festivals such as the Columbus Arts Festival along the Scioto River. Old neighborhoods, like German Village, preserve the city's past. Columbus is a modern city that is full of history!

COLUMBUS ARTS FESTIVAL

GERMAN VILLAGE

17

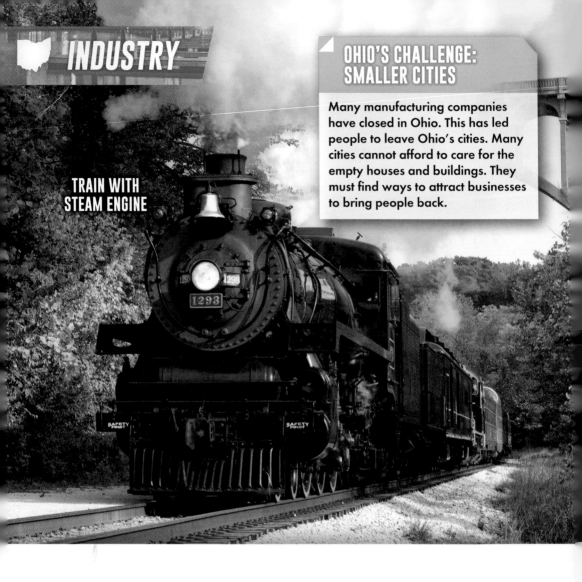

INDUSTRY

OHIO'S CHALLENGE: SMALLER CITIES

Many manufacturing companies have closed in Ohio. This has led people to leave Ohio's cities. Many cities cannot afford to care for the empty houses and buildings. They must find ways to attract businesses to bring people back.

TRAIN WITH STEAM ENGINE

In the 1800s, Ohio was an important trade center. Its **natural resources** and location on Lake Erie drew many people. Farmers grew corn, wheat, and other grains. People traveled and traded along Ohio's **canals**, railways, and roads. Coal mines increased as **steam engines** became common in boats, trains, and factories. Ohio's factories produced foods, glass, rubber, and machine parts.

Manufacturing is still important, but Ohio has fewer factories today. Factories now make cars, aircraft, or other machines. Most people have service jobs. Many work in health care and education. Ohio farmers are some of the top soybean producers in the country.

RUBBER CAPITAL OF THE WORLD

Akron, Ohio, was once known as the Rubber Capital of the World. It was home to many rubber factories. Four tire companies once did business there!

INVENTED IN OHIO

PORTABLE VACUUM CLEANER
Date Invented: 1907
Inventor: James Murray Spangler

LIFE SAVERS CANDIES
Date Invented: 1912
Inventor: Clarence Crane

CASH REGISTER
Date Patented: 1879
Inventor: James Ritty

SUPERMAN COMICS
Date Invented: 1938
Inventors: Jerry Siegel and Joe Shuster

POLISH *KIELBASA*

Ohio's foods come from many backgrounds. Italian and Polish foods are popular in Cleveland. People love Italian ice and Polish *kielbasa*. Clambakes are a favorite fall dish. People steam clams, chicken, corn, and potatoes in one pot!

CHEESE, PLEASE!

Swiss cheese has been made in Ohio for more than 100 years. The state's Swiss cheese factories make millions of pounds of cheese each year!

In Cincinnati, people love German foods. Many people eat *goetta* for breakfast. German immigrants created this sausage. Chili is Cincinnati's most famous dish. It is served over spaghetti noodles and topped with cheese! For dessert, many Ohioans enjoy buckeyes, which are peanut butter balls dipped in chocolate. They are made to look like the buckeye nut!

CINCINNATI CHILI

BUCKEYES

Have an adult help you make this recipe!

MAKES ABOUT 30

INGREDIENTS
1 1/2 cups peanut butter
1 cup softened butter
1/2 teaspoon vanilla extract
6 cups confectioners' sugar
4 cups chocolate chips

DIRECTIONS
1. In a large bowl, mix the peanut butter, butter, vanilla, and confectioners' sugar.
2. Roll the mixture into balls about 1 inch (2.5 centimeters) across. Place on a cookie sheet lined with parchment paper.
3. Poke a toothpick into each peanut butter ball. Chill in the freezer until firm.
4. Melt the chocolate chips in the microwave. Stir every 30 seconds until smooth.
5. Using the toothpicks as handles, dip each peanut butter ball into the melted chocolate. Leave some peanut butter showing so that the treat looks like a buckeye.
6. Refrigerate the buckeyes until the chocolate has hardened. Enjoy!

LAKE ERIE

There is a lot to do in Ohio! In the summer, people hike and camp in Ohio's state parks. Lake Erie is a popular place to swim, boat, and fish. In winter, Ohioans love to go skiing and sledding.

22

Ohio hosts many theater events and concerts. Karamu House is famous for its plays celebrating Black culture. COSI in Columbus welcomes people to learn about space and technology. Sports fans have a lot of teams to cheer on. Everyone roots for the Ohio State Buckeyes football team in the fall. Ohio also has professional teams in every major sport!

TALE OF TWO FOOTBALL TEAMS

Ohio has two professional football teams. The Cincinnati Bengals and Cleveland Browns both have large followings.

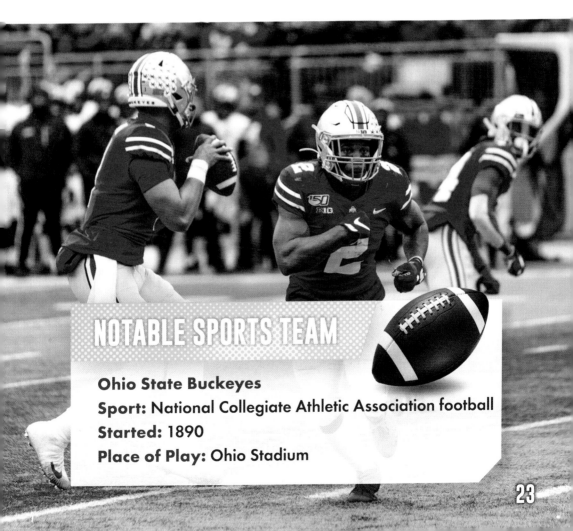

NOTABLE SPORTS TEAM

Ohio State Buckeyes
Sport: National Collegiate Athletic Association football
Started: 1890
Place of Play: Ohio Stadium

VECTREN DAYTON
AIR SHOW

Ohioans enjoy fun festivals all year. Cleveland's Rock and Roll Hall of Fame adds new musicians in an annual event. People gather at the Vectren Dayton Air Show every summer. They watch planes loop across the sky. Akron hosts the All-American Soap Box Derby each July. Kids race each other in small, unpowered race cars.

ALL-AMERICAN
SOAP BOX DERBY

The Ohio State Fair happens in late summer in Columbus. The fair has food, rides, concerts, and art. In October, Ohioans eat German foods at the Ohio Sauerkraut Festival in Waynesville. Ohioans love gathering to celebrate what makes their state great!

JOHNNY APPLESEED

Johnny Appleseed planted apple trees across Ohio in the 1800s. The small town of Lisbon celebrates Ohio's apples with the Johnny Appleseed Festival every September!

OHIO STATE FAIR

OHIO TIMELINE

1795

The Treaty of Greenville forces the Miami, Shawnee, and other Native American groups to give up most of their Ohio land

MID-1600S

French explorers become the first Europeans to reach what is now Ohio

1803

Ohio becomes the 17th state

1763

The French and Indian War puts Ohio under British control

1783

The U.S. takes control of Ohio when the Revolutionary War ends

1861-1865

Ohio sends around 320,000 troops to support the Union in the U.S. Civil War

1995

Cleveland's Rock and Roll
Hall of Fame opens

2016

The Cleveland Cavaliers
defeat the Golden State
Warriors to win their first
NBA championship

2003

An error at an electric company in Akron
causes 50 million people to lose electricity
in the Northeast Blackout

1902

Ohio's state flag is adopted

Nicknames: The Buckeye State,
The Mother of Presidents, The Heart of It All

Motto: With God, All Things Are Possible

Date of Statehood: March 1, 1803 (the 17th state)

Capital City: Columbus ★

Other Major Cities: Cleveland, Cincinnati, Toledo, Akron, Dayton

Area: 44,826 square miles (116,099 square kilometers);
Ohio is the 34th largest state.

Population

11,799,448

(2020)

STATE FLAG

Ohio's flag is the only state flag that does not have a rectangular shape. The right side tapers to a V-shaped space called a swallowtail. The flag is white with a red stripe at the top, middle, and bottom. The left side has a large blue triangle. In the middle is a red circle with a white border. It looks like an O for Ohio. Around the circle, 17 white stars show Ohio's place as the 17th state.

INDUSTRY

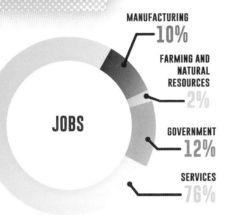

MANUFACTURING
10%

FARMING AND NATURAL RESOURCES
2%

JOBS

GOVERNMENT
12%

SERVICES
76%

Main Exports

machinery

medical devices

aircraft

plastic products

cars

iron and steel

Natural Resources
coal, oil, natural gas, salt

GOVERNMENT

17 ELECTORAL VOTES

Federal Government
15 | 2
REPRESENTATIVES | SENATORS

USA

OH

State Government
99 | 33
REPRESENTATIVES | SENATORS

STATE SYMBOLS

STATE BIRD
NORTHERN CARDINAL

STATE ANIMAL
WHITE-TAILED DEER

STATE FLOWER
RED CARNATION

STATE TREE
OHIO BUCKEYE

GLOSSARY

ancestors—relatives who lived long ago

canals—human-made waterways that boats can travel through

confluence—the place where two rivers meet

continental—referring to a climate that has hot summers and cold winters, such as those found in central North America and Asia

culture—the beliefs, arts, and ways of life in a place or society

distinct—different from others

ethnic—related to a group of people who share customs and an identity

gorge—a narrow canyon with steep walls

humid—having a lot of moisture in the air

immigrants—people who move to a new country

manufacturing—a field of work in which people use machines to make products

Midwest—a region of 12 states in the north-central United States

natural resources—materials in the earth that are taken out and used to make products or fuel

plains—large areas of flat land

plateau—an area of flat, raised land

preserve—to keep something in its original state

reservations—areas of land that are controlled by Native American tribes

Revolutionary War—the war from 1775 to 1783 in which the United States fought for independence from Great Britain

service jobs—jobs that perform tasks for people or businesses

settlers—people who move to live in a new, undeveloped region

steam engines—engines that generate power with steam

urban—related to cities and city life

AT THE LIBRARY

Gitlin, Marty. *Ohio.* North Mankato, Minn.:
Children's Press, 2019.

Kortemeier, Todd. *It's Great to Be a Fan in Ohio.*
Lake Elmo, Minn.: Focus Readers, 2019.

Mattern, Joanne. *Cuyahoga Valley.* New York, N.Y.:
Children's Press, 2019.

ON THE WEB

FACTSURFER

Factsurfer.com gives you
a safe, fun way to find
more information.

1. Go to www.factsurfer.com.

2. Enter "Ohio" into the search box
   and click 🔍.

3. Select your book cover to see a list
   of related content.

INDEX